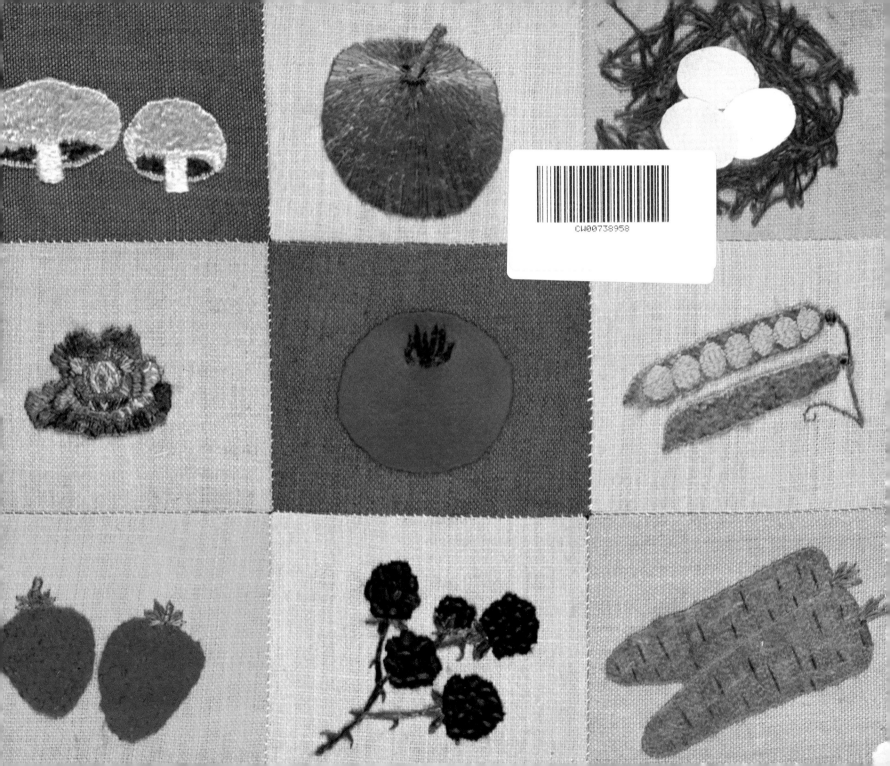

British Library Cataloguing
in Publication Data
Youngs, Betty
Pink pigs in mud.
1. Colour – Juvenile literature
I. Title
535.6   QC495.5
ISBN 0–370–30344–X

Copyright © Betty Youngs 1982
Printed in Great Britain for
The Bodley Head,
32 Bedford Square, London WC1B 3EL
by W. S. Cowell Ltd, Ipswich
First published 1982
Reprinted 1985, 1987

**OTHER PICTURE BOOKS
BY BETTY YOUNGS**

**Humpty Dumpty and Other First Rhymes
One Panda: An Animal Counting Book
Two by Two**

Pink Pigs in Mud

a Colour Book by
Betty Youngs

THE BODLEY HEAD
London

Ted Hollins has a farm
and on it there are

green
frogs
by the
pond

grey
donkeys
under
a tree

red
poppies
in the
cornfield

brown
owls
in the
wood

yellow
chicks
in grass

pink
pigs
in mud

white
sheep
on a
hill

orange
carrots
in a
basket

black
horse
in the
meadow

and a big
blue
tractor
in the yard.

Which colours can you see in this picture?